Ancient Dartmoor

AN INTRODUCTION

PAUL WHITE

Bossiney Books

This reprint 2018
First published 2000 by Bossiney Books Ltd
67 West Busk Lane, Otley, LS21 3LY
ISBN 978-1-899383-22-1
© 2000 Paul White All rights reserved
Photographs by the author except that on page 15 which is by Matt Devenish
Printed in Great Britain by R Booth Ltd, Penryn, Cornwall

The conventional 'Ages' of prehistory

Palaeolithic (= Old Stone Age) prior to c.8000 BC
This term covers half a million years of complex hominid development. I am relieved to say it is not relevant to this book!

Mesolithic (= Middle Stone Age) c.8000–4500 BC
The period following the last Ice Age, when people lived in Britain as nomadic hunter-gatherers.

Neolithic (= New Stone Age) c.4500–c.2200 BC
The beginning of farming, and therefore of settlements, first with the control of animal herds, then development of crop growing.

The Bronze Age c.2200–700 BC
Metal working had begun, but made only a limited impact. Society seems to have become more politically organised.

The Iron Age c.700 BC–400 AD
The use of iron affected everyday life profoundly, and not always for the best. Ploughshares were all too often beaten into swords. The Romans came in AD 43 – but had little impact on Dartmoor.

These 'Ages' of prehistory are artificial divisions which originated in the nineteenth century, and archaeological knowledge has come a long way since then. Early archaeologists envisaged a series of invasions each bringing a 'superior' technology, whereas subsequent archaeology envisaged peoples mainly staying put and ideas (technological, economic and political) doing the moving, perhaps accompanied by small numbers of migrants.

In 2018 this debate was restarted by major new DNA evidence.

The terms are therefore not entirely satisfactory today, but they are still used. The dates given are *very* approximate, as developments occurred at different times in different regions, and one period shaded imperceptibly into another. In particular the Late Neolithic/Early Bronze Age on Dartmoor was really a continuum, and the acronym 'LANEBA' is sometimes used.

Natural rock and ancient house walls merge as one

Introduction

Almost everywhere you walk on Dartmoor you will find evidence of earlier people – burial mounds, stone rows, stone circles and ancient settlements. Even the glorious scenery, which seems utterly 'natural', is to a large extent the result of human interference. Prehistoric and medieval farmers, and later tinners and quarrymen, have all made a significant impact on what can be seen today.

Because they built in stone, and because later generations did not choose to re-use the same sites, much remains which in other areas may once have existed but has left no trace.

There have been four main periods in which people have found it worthwhile to colonise the Dartmoor uplands in large numbers, and much longer periods when the moor was mainly used for summer pasturing of animals, sometimes brought from a great distance.

The main periods of farming colonisation were:
1. The Neolithic
2. The Middle Bronze Age, particularly 1800–1200 BC
3. The medieval period, particularly AD 1200–1350
4. The early nineteenth century

The first two periods are covered in this book, the latter two in *Dartmoor's History*.

The Neolithic

Six or seven thousand years ago the landscape of Dartmoor was quite unlike what we see today. It is known from the pollen record that it was mainly wooded, up to a tree line at around 460 metres (1500 ft). The dominant tree species were oak and alder. Doubtless many of the oaks were stunted, as their direct descendants still are at Wistman's Wood, but the weather was generally warmer and drier, and the soil was not the pervasive peat which it is today.

There were people in this landscape. For thousands of years men had roamed in search of deer and other wild animals, while the women and children gathered edible fruits and grains. (Perhaps there were people who transcended the gender roles, but they would have been exceptional.) This nomadic life of hunter-gatherers was typical of the Mesolithic.

Around 5000 BC a major change occurred, as people began to try to control their environment. The pollen record shows a decline in woodland and an increase in grasses, and then in heathers. Forest fires were deliberately started by the late Mesolithic hunters so that the deer would be attracted by better grazing, and be more easily taken than in the wooded areas.

The next stage marked the beginning of the Neolithic. On Dartmoor this occurred around 4500 BC. Semi-permanent settlements were founded, based on pastoral farming, with some hunting and gathering but from a fixed base.

Not long after this came mankind's most revolutionary invention ever, arable farming; though perhaps it is more likely that it was not the men but the women, already responsible for gathering, who discovered the advantages of sowing and planting crops rather than wandering for miles hoping to find them. People began, in a more or less literal sense, to put down roots.

The beginning of agriculture, and the increasingly settled life which followed, permitted more sophisticated social structures to evolve.

White Tor fort, believed to be Neolithic in origin

Nomadic life did not cease overnight. The primitive agricultural technique known as 'slash-and-burn' involves making a clearing in the forest which, for a time, is capable of growing crops; but since techniques of manuring and composting had not been discovered, the fertility of the soil rapidly deteriorated, and a new clearing had to be made.

The abandoned clearing did not regenerate as woodland, because the saplings were eaten by deer. Far from having an instinctive understanding of sustainable agriculture, these early farmers started a process of soil impoverishment which led to deep peat deposits covering much of the moor, making it impossible for all but the most specialist plant species to survive.

Although finds of Neolithic flint implements are quite common, identified settlement sites from this period are not. Only two are known, both of them defended sites, at White Tor and the Dewerstone rock. Warfare or cattle-rustling seems to have been a feature of late Neolithic life.

The limitations of archaeological knowledge

1. Archaeologists can only find what is there to be found – which means it had to be left around in the first place, and then to have been able to survive.

2. Whilst stone survives, wood and bone often do not, especially in the acidic moorland soils. Paradoxically, while Dartmoor offers the non-archaeologist a nearly unique chance to experience the past in the form of undisturbed domestic and ceremonial remains, it frustrates the professionals because the kinds of find they need for radio-carbon dating and for interpretation have been destroyed by the acids.

3. Our understanding of the past must allow for what we cannot now find. Dartmoor and the Cornish uplands seem to have been intensively farmed, whilst the lowlands are devoid of remains. But this may be because lowland structures were made of wood. Even if they were in stone, stone is a valuable resource and would have been re-used by later inhabitants. The upland structures remain because there were very few later inhabitants.

4. It is impossible to judge when a lump of granite was quarried by looking at it, or even by scientific tests. In the past some structures have been misinterpreted as ancient which were really quite modern, or even of natural origin, and some diggings represent the work of tomb-robbers or early antiquarians rather than prehistoric people! Who can say whether such misinterpretation is not still happening?

5. Interpretation of visible remains is not always easy. Even to an expert eye, apparently, a ruined ring cairn can be indistinguishable from a ruined hut or a small stone circle.

6. Modern archaeology is a slow and painstaking task, and in consequence expensive. It also destroys the site, leaving nothing intact for future generations.

This stone is now known to have been destined for a cider press, but never completed. An early archaeologist unfortunately mistook it for a chambered tomb or 'cromlech' – a classic of misinterpretation

It is just possible that some of the stone hut circles are also Neolithic in origin, and those few that have been excavated by modern methods have shown signs of being built over earlier wooden buildings. Oak was still plentiful on Dartmoor in the Neolithic, and it is likely that buildings and fences were more easily constructed in wood than in stone.

For the reasons explained in the panel, dating of Dartmoor's hut circles and ceremonial sites (stone rows, circles, cairns and standing stones) is most uncertain. In many cases it is not known whether a feature is Neolithic or much later.

There are a small number of chambered tombs (they used to be called 'cromlechs') which are definitely Neolithic, probably earlier than 3000 BC, most notably Spinsters' Rock and the damaged tomb at Corringdon Ball. They resemble the 'quoits' of west Cornwall and consisted of a substantial stone chamber, sometimes with a stone passage for access, covered by a long mound of stones or earth.

Spinsters' Rock, not far from Castle Drogo. This really is a Neolithic chambered tomb, and not an apple crusher! It would originally have been covered with a mound of earth or stones

Some of the stone rows, of which there are around 80 known on Dartmoor and perhaps more waiting below the peat to be discovered, are probably late Neolithic or early Bronze Age, from around 2200 BC. One recently discovered row has been dated to 3500 BC.

These rows are often associated with round cairns and long-stones ('menhirs') and some of these also may be of the same period.

There are many questions to be answered about the development of the cultures which built these monuments, and they are far from being resolved, certainly in respect of Dartmoor where dating evidence is mostly lacking. For those of us who are not archaeologists, these difficulties of interpretation need not spoil our enjoyment of the sites. It is probably sufficient to know that the majority of the prehistoric remains still visible date from the period 2200–1200 BC, the Bronze Age.

The Bronze Age

This period has left an astonishing amount of evidence on Dartmoor, most of it exposed to the view of the casual visitor. It is calculated that there are some 5000 'hut circles' surviving, some standing alone, others in complex village settlements of sixty or more huts. Not all the huts were occupied at the same time, and some were out-buildings rather than dwellings, but there were wooden buildings as well as stone ones. At its peak, the moorland population may have neared 10,000, at least in summer.

As well as the settlements, there are ceremonial complexes with numerous stone rows (single rows, double rows or multiple rows), stone circles, standing stones and various cairns, some containing 'cists' (from *kist ven,* 'stone chest' in Cornish) which held a burial.

Whilst the stone rows do not compare in grandeur with those at Carnac in Brittany, and the stone circles do not compare in scale with Stonehenge or Avebury, they are in many ways more evocative, just as a remote rural church may be more evocative than the bustle of St Peter's in Rome or of Westminster Abbey. You can walk around and through these Dartmoor monuments, touch the stones, and be alone, which you cannot do at the greater sites.

Alone with the stones, at Stalldown near Cornwood

Looking south from near Combestone Tor. The 'co-axial' pattern of reaves can best be seen when the sun is low in the sky

Even more remarkable in some ways than the ceremonial sites are the field boundaries, which were only recognised as Bronze Age in the 1970s. Prior to that, archaeologists specialising in prehistory assumed they were medieval, and the medievalists assumed they were prehistoric, so both groups ignored them! They are known by the local dialect word 'reave', a boundary (compare 'riven in two') and they seem to have been built in a flurry of construction around 1500 BC, perhaps when 'the Beaker People' arrived in numbers.

These reaves are low banks of stone (or earth where stone is not available), often many kilometres long and frequently laid out in dead straight lines. Sometimes they occur in parallel systems (technically known as 'co-axial') accurate to within 1°, even though they cross hilly country. Such accuracy would be an achievement even for a modern surveyor, and only today can it be fully appreciated, from maps and aerial photographs. Reaves tend to be just over a metre wide, but only about 30-40 cm high, certainly not high enough to keep animals from crossing them. Probably they were topped by

It is surprisingly easy to miss reaves when you are close to them. A reave extends from the bottom left of this photograph up to the left of Kestor, and its path is marked as much by the line of scrub as by visible stones

thorn bushes, rather like a low 'Cornish hedge', or else the animals were controlled by wattle fences or rows of dead thorn bushes.

Although many of the surviving settlements are on land which has been abandoned by farmers except as rough grazing, the field systems established in the Bronze Age have sometimes been fossilised in 'modern' field systems well beyond the moorland boundary.

In other words, some Devon farms have straight boundaries created 3500 years ago. Parish boundaries too sometimes follow ancient reaves: much of Ilsington's parish boundary, for example, may be identical with that of the village which was its Bronze Age predecessor, though it is not known whether there was continuity, or whether the Saxons just used the ancient reave as a useful boundary when they came to create the parish.

Were some of the farming routines of medieval times also perhaps relics of the way of life in the Bronze Age?

If we imagine Dartmoor as a massive cake, domed in the middle, then the archetypal Dartmoor border parish is like a slice of the cake – except that the slice doesn't extend all the way to the middle. A roughly circular area in the middle of the cake, the highest and least attractive ground for farming, is the 'Forest' of central Dartmoor – forest in this sense being a Norman legal term which had nothing to do with woodland. (Once the parish system was in full effect, all land had to be assigned to one, and the whole of the Forest was assigned rather absurdly to Lydford parish.)

In Saxon times the high moor which was to become the Forest seems to have belonged to no one, and been used as summer grazing by herdsmen from all over Devon. In spring they would take their animals up ancient drove roads (some of which remain as green lanes) between or through the parishes.

The Normans, in contrast, were in no doubt that all land belonged

This reave is part of the co-axial field pattern of the Kestor settlement, and includes what appears to be a paved gateway

This is a Bronze Age drove road, some 3500 years old, which gave access from the lowlands to the high moor, but kept the passing animals out of the neighbouring fields. It can be traced for at least 200 metres, and lies on Hayne Down at SX 745802, within 500 metres of Bowerman's Nose but much less often visited. Some of the green lanes which continue as footpaths or bridleways to this day may have origins just as ancient

to the king, but even under the Normans the Forest still retained some curious legal characteristics.

The medieval Dartmoor parishes had their main village fields just off the moor, at the outer and lower end of their 'slice'. This was also where most parishioners lived. Above these fields, on the outer rim of the moor, was the common land of the village, within which each villager had defined rights, and above that again was the unenclosed open moorland to which individual parishioners had no special claim. This may have been a system in continuous use since the Bronze Age.

The Bronze Age settlements fall into two main groupings. On the southern and eastern sides of the moor, there are massive field systems defined by reaves, where hut circles are placed within the fields. As with the later parishes, these settlements tend to be at the lower end of the field system, each with access to a river. The parallel reaves stretch upwards towards the higher ground, with cross-reaves defining squarish fields at the lower end, then much longer fields, and at the top of the system a major reave cutting off the Bronze Age 'parish' from the ancient equivalent of the Forest.

It is tempting to assume that the squarish lower fields were used for crops and the longer rectangular fields were used for grazing, and that as the population grew, so the settlers would bring more land under cultivation.

A second and very different style of farming is suggested by other settlements which consist of 'pounds', walled enclosures usually with hut circles within them. These can vary from a simple wall round a single hut to an incredibly complex design of interlocking rings containing as many as 60 huts.

An idyllic place for a settlement, in the lower Erme valley not far above Ivybridge, its fields here smothered by bluebells

The most famous of the pound settlements is Grimspound, which is untypical in the immense thickness of its outer walls. It has been calculated that these would have taken 35 man-years to make. Since the site is badly positioned for defence (and the Bronze Age was a remarkably peaceful period) it is hard to see why such a massive structure was needed

These settlements tend to be on higher ground, and in this case the temptation is to assume these people were pastoralists, keeping their cattle or sheep on the moor but sometimes bringing them in for protection from raiders such as wolves or the wild lads from the next valley. The problem is that there is virtually no evidence for these tempting assumptions. The only pound to have been properly excavated was at Shaugh Moor, prior to its destruction by the china clay industry. It proved to have no entrance gate in the outer wall. Instead there was a stile – so the wall must have been to keep animals out rather than to enclose them.

A field which has been grazed is usually high in phosphates as a result of the droppings: there was no evidence that the pound had

Remains of a fairly typical hut at Stalldown in the Erme valley

been grazed. Presumably the inside of the pound was a garden for vegetables or corn.

Other pound hamlets may have had different farming methods. Certainly many have entrance ways, though none are as large as that at Grimspound, the most visited of these settlements.

Archaeologists analysing the designs of hut circles have come up with many types, but to the casual visitor they tend at first to look rather similar. Size is very varied, from a diameter of 1.5 m to as much as 11 m. The size of house you lived in may have depended on age or marital status rather than on wealth. The average field-system hut is larger than the average pound hut. Were the inhabitants richer? Were the pound huts seasonal shelters for herdsmen?

The largest hut in a settlement is often separated from the others. Probably it was the chief's house, but it might have been a debating chamber for the local council or the village hall for Bronze Age quiz evenings. It is easy to make guesses about ancient social arrangements and politics, but in reality the evidence just is not there.

The Round Pound – a misleading name because it is the largest hut within the Kestor co-axial field system, but was surrounded by a substantial wall. Excavated in 1951, it was found to have been re-occupied by early medieval iron-workers, and later by a shepherd

Huts could be rebuilt many times over, and were sometimes reduced in size in their later rebuilding. This was perhaps because roof timber of the right length could no longer be obtained, once there was little woodland left, but the date of such rebuildings is unknown, and may even have been a thousand years later: sometimes medieval tinners patched up a Bronze Age hut.

Some huts have hearths (oak charcoal has been found during excavations), some have inside benches, one even has a stone cupboard. The entrances generally face downhill, and are often southeast or south-west facing. The door posts may still be standing. A very small proportion have a porch to divert the wind, but a larger number have some paving at the entrance, and even paved drainage for storm water. The floor was generally made of gravel, though sometimes paved or cobbled.

It is assumed that the hut roof was conical, made of wood, supported inside by one or more upright posts, and thatched. What we see is only the bare skeleton of the building, and as originally constructed and decorated it was probably no worse a home than many rural dwellings as late as the nineteenth century.

Apart from the huts which have been robbed of stone for much later field walls, some were demolished in their own time. This was not always done for the stone. Sometimes the purpose was apparently to render them uninhabitable, and occasionally the stone has been piled in the middle to create a cairn, though because skeletons have not survived in Dartmoor's acid soils, it is impossible to know whether the occupant was buried in it.

Only a couple of dozen huts have been excavated using modern methods, but the results have been generally disappointing, revealing very few artefacts or items suitable for radio-carbon dating. These ancient people seem to have been excessively houseproud from an archaeologist's point of view – quite unlike their medieval

This is a piece of (relatively) modern walling. If the smaller, lighter, stones were removed and the larger stones slumped to the ground, the result might well resemble the hut and cairn remains which survive. The ancient structures were better built than might now appear

This is the robbed cairn at the end of the Hingston Hill stone row which was heavily restored in 1894. It is sometimes difficult to tell an unrestored robbed cairn from a hut circle, since in both cases the first stage was to make a ring of upright stones around the outside. And the ring of stones remaining from a large cairn can look very similar to a small stone circle. Perhaps their builders made a symbolic connection between these forms as a house for the dead?

successors, whose slovenly habits have left much to reveal their life-styles! Perhaps they occupied these huts in summer only, and gave them a very thorough spring-clean?

Something which everyone would love to find is conclusive evidence that the Bronze Age inhabitants of Dartmoor were streaming for tin – which is one of the metals used to make bronze. Many settlements are alongside later tin streamworks, but these worked the ground so thoroughly that no evidence of any earlier working could be left, except perhaps tools, and those may still be buried under tons of waste rock. There have been finds of tiny amounts of tin slag in a hut, but this might have been left by a later occupant. No bronze artefact demonstrably made on Dartmoor is as yet known.

The ceremonial monuments

We shall never know what the importance of stone circles or stone rows was to the people who built them. It is hard not to believe that they had some religious significance, but what that religion might have been and what ceremonies might have been performed is a matter almost entirely of guesswork.

Rows, circles and menhirs may all have been constructed in wood in earlier times, and perhaps continued to be so in lowland areas. Sacred glades were certainly a feature of British religion in the time of the Romans; that was more than 1500 years later and there may have been no continuity, but it is possible that to the ancient people the menhirs symbolised sacred trees and the circle a glade.

The Dartmoor Exploration Committee excavated several circles between 1894 and 1904 (when techniques were still primitive in the extreme) and found charcoal. That might imply either funeral pyres or midsummer bonfires.

The Drizzlecombe stone row

Above: Scorhill stone circle

Below: The Hurston Ridge double stone row, with 49 pairs of stones

The 'Nine Stones' at Belstone looks like a stone circle but was actually a ring of stones around a cairn. Such cairn rings were sometimes part of the cairn structure, but sometimes formed a decoration around it

Buried within a cairn there was usually a 'cist' – a stone chest in which was placed either the body or its ashes. Valuable grave goods were sometimes included, which led to most of the cairns being plundered and damaged within the last thousand years. Sometimes as here no trace of the actual cairn survives

'Hillson's house' cairn. In the middle is a hut, built within the cairn according to legend by a man called Hillson who was a manufacturer of eight-day clocks

Detail of a cairn on Hingston Hill. Some archaeologists think they can see signs of a chambered structure, others think it never was more than a pile of stones, some of which may have been robbed

One of the six stone rows in the Shovel Down ceremonial complex leads up to this 'fourfold circle'. This is a cairn at the foundation of which were four concentric stone rings

The stone rows often lead upward to a burial cairn or cairns, and sometimes there is a menhir or a blocking stone at the lower end. But there is such enormous variety in the number of rows, the size of stones, and the orientation, width and length of the 'avenue' (from a few metres to 3.3 km or 2 miles) that it is hard to see any consistent pattern. The rows seem to invite upward procession, and excavation of double rows elsewhere has apparently suggested that people processed outside the stones: perhaps the spirits of the ancestors processed inside the row...

There are certain sites which seem to have been more important (more sacred?) than others, because several monuments are combined in a 'ceremonial complex'. The easiest to explore is that at Merrivale, but those at Drizzlecombe on the upper Plym and at Shovel Down on Chagford Common are particularly fine.

Above: One of the double rows at Shovel Down

At Drizzlecombe each of three stone rows has a longstone at the lower end and a cairn at the upper end. This longstone stands 4.2 metres high

Merrivale ceremonial complex, very easily approached from the Tavistock-Princetown road. The road itself runs through an ancient village, to which the ceremonial complex presumably belonged

One well publicised theory is that the monuments were astronomical observatories. Just possibly they were, but personally I find the evidence unconvincing. Very many of the stones lay flat and partly-hidden in Victorian times, and were re-erected by well-meaning enthusiasts – not necessarily in their original positions and sometimes with a few added to fill in the gaps. The result is a much more atmospheric and awe-inspiring monument, but not absolutely authentic. Any sight-lines to celestial events are likely to be there more by chance than by design.

My own advice would be not to bother about their unknowable purpose but to visit some of the best examples and soak in the atmosphere. However, if you just pick a monument at random from the OS map to visit, you may be disappointed: some of them have stones so small that they are invisible under the bracken in summer.

The historical sequence

The lack of radio-carbon dates, and the general scarcity of other evidence, makes it difficult to piece together what may have happened and when, but it does seem likely that the Neolithic inhabitants were partially withdrawing from the moor around 3000 BC, because at that time there was some regeneration of woodland.

What appears to be another people, known from their distinctive pottery as the Beaker people, come into the scene in the early Bronze Age, around 2200 BC, when they would have found the uplands relatively empty. These people built cairns and stone rows. When the stone row at Cholwichtown was excavated (prior to destruction by a china clay pit) the results were rather disappointing, but it was shown to have been constructed within a woodland clearing which had previously been used for growing cereals.

Piles Hill stone row requires imagination. Many of the stones lie flat and some are invisible. It is unusual in several ways and may be older than most other rows: the stones are very large, it runs east-west (most of its neighbours run north-south) and across the ridge-line rather than up the slope

The early settlers built wooden houses, but the first stone houses may be as early as 1800 BC. The farmers probably used wooden hurdles to control their stock, but also constructed some early reaves.

From around 1700 BC the population rose, and suddenly around 1500 BC there seems to have been a large simultaneous influx, possibly a whole tribe arriving together. These people had the expertise to build vast accurate field systems. In total there are over 400 km of reaves. The largest field system covers no less than 20 km^2 and includes 25 separate hut groups. This was a complex and sophisticated society, with some kind of central planning and control going way beyond that of individual villages.

Both the quality of the planning and the undisputed power to put it into practice suggests a 'state' on at least a regional scale. There is no suggestion during the whole of this period of any warfare, in contrast to the periods before and after. The reaves would have required specialist surveyors directing the operation of the whole community. Different work gangs produced each section, with varying degrees of competence, which suggests that these reaves were all constructed in a single operation. At the same time, from the pollen evidence, very large numbers of trees were felled.

The pound dwellers on the higher land may have been present before the arrival of the 'reave-builders', and in some cases old pounds are actually accommodated within the field system, so some of the earlier inhabitants may have been displaced.

The two kinds of community, one based on pounds in the uplands, the other on field systems a little lower down, seem to have co-existed harmoniously, but their inter-relationship can only be guessed at. Did they mix socially? Did they inter-marry? Could a man or woman decide which way of life they preferred?

Such interesting human questions will probably never be answered, though archaeologists may yet discover more about the economic relationships within this society.

The end of Bronze Age Dartmoor

From a peak around 1300 BC, the population seems to have dropped, but how rapidly, or why, remains uncertain. The most probable reasons would include worsening in the weather patterns and gradual impoverishment of the soil, over-cropped and over-grazed by the rapidly increasing population. These factors could have made it worthwhile to move to the lowlands, even if they had yet to be cleared of woodland.

There is evidence that some settlements were deserted in a hurry, with valuables left behind in the huts. This could indicate warfare, but if the 'tribe' moved onto Dartmoor in a single migration, perhaps they moved out in the same way, and some of the inhabitants may have received little notice.

Sudden disaster has also been conjectured, a plague perhaps, or the eruption of an Icelandic volcano called Hekla, in the twelfth century BC, which may have affected the climate or produced acid rain.

Prehistoric people were not exempt from the natural rise and fall which affects the population of any species. A famine or a plague could reduce their numbers. In some cases it might be hundreds of years before the population would again recover.

What is certain is that the upland farms were deserted around that time, as were similar holdings elsewhere in England. Some of the lower farms may have been continuously occupied ever since, but any evidence of the Neolithic or Bronze Age settlers will then have been destroyed by more recent occupation.

The Iron Age

Iron was introduced from about 700 BC and was much cheaper to make than bronze. Ordinary people had no bronze farm implements: they continued to rely on stone tools, which by this time were very sophisticated. It was iron which brought the use of metal to the ordinary family.

Hembury hill-fort is Iron Age, but was refortified with this Norman motte in the middle of the older earthworks

Possibly because the weather at this period was too wet to allow crops to ripen, the upland farms remained deserted, except for summer grazing, which continued uninterrupted.

A few earlier huts were reoccupied, either by farmers or by metal workers, and a few new huts were built within old field walls. It is only recently that totally trustworthy evidence of iron-working on Dartmoor in the Roman period has emerged, but in general this must have been a miserable time for the moor's inhabitants.

None of this left much archaeological record, and indeed there are no upland sites of any general interest dating from the whole period 1000 BC to AD 1000.

There are a number of Iron Age defended sites on the periphery of the Moor, of which the most interesting is Hembury hill-fort (SX 726684), which was refortified as a motte-and-bailey castle in the Middle Ages, but to my mind these earthworks lack the magic of the ancient stones of high Dartmoor.

Some of the most enjoyable places to visit:

Chambered tombs

Corringdon Ball (669613). Impressive, if damaged. Park as near as you can to (684602) and walk up an archetypal drove road.

Spinsters' Rock (702908). Impressive structure, away from the Moor in field near farm (access often muddy). No walk involved.

Ceremonial complexes

Merrivale (555748). Several 🅿 nearby. Particularly short walk. Bronze Age settlement between stone rows and road.

Drizzlecombe (591670). 🅿 at (577673). Surrounded by settlements. Medium length walk.

Shovel Down (660859). 🅿 at (662866). Don't miss fascinating co-axial field system centred on (665865) and Round Pound (664869). A longish walk could include Scorhill stone circle.

Stone rows

Hingston Hill (588693). 🅿 at (568693). Terminal cairn. Other cairns nearby. Also known as Down Tor row. A lovely walk.

Piles Hill (655611). If you park at Stowford Bridge (641568) you can take in the lengthy Butterdon Hill stone row on your way. Be warned, the Piles Hill row is unrestored and requires some imagination. A longish walk.

Stalldown (632623). 🅿 at (627613). On the same medium length walk you can include Hillson's House cairn (637623) and a Bronze Age settlement at (637612).

Stone circles

Grey Wethers (639831). Park at Postbridge. A longish walk.

Langstone Moor (556782). 🅿 at (521779). Within Range Area, so check on firing times! The walk can take in White Tor fort, the Langstone, and its associated stone row – if you can find it!

Scorhill (655874). 🅿 at (661878).

Settlements

Foales Arishes, settlement and co-axial field system (738759).
🅿 at (742761). Very short walk.

Grimspound, pound settlement (701809). 🅿 at (697809). Very
short walk. Much visited, deservedly so.

Kestor settlement and field system (665865). 🅿 at (662866).

Other

Hayne Down, Bronze Age drove road (745802). Park as near as you
can to (739800) but try not to inconvenience other traffic.

Hembury fort, Iron Age/Norman (725684). 🅿 at (724688).

White Tor, fort, probably Neolithic (542787). 🅿 at (521779).
Within Range Area, so check on firing times! See also Langstone
stone circle. Interesting pound settlement at (540785).

Further reading

Probably the most readable Dartmoor book by an archaeologist is
Sandy Gerrard's *English Heritage Book of Dartmoor Landscapes
through Time*, BT Batsford/English Heritage 1997. If you really get
interested you will want Jeremy Butler's wonderful and
comprehensive *Dartmoor Atlas of Antiquities*, in five volumes,
Devon Books 1991-7. Volume 5 is a summary of 'The Second
Millennium BC' and can be consulted independently of the others.